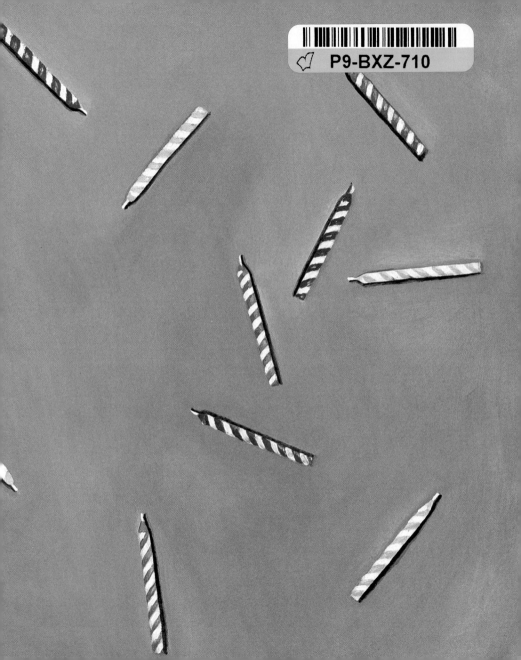

I LIKED YOU AT TEN
I'll Like You Again

REFLECTIONS OF "MOMMY" YEARS

Written by P. Taylor Copeland
Illustrated by Suzi Bliss Kyle

I Liked You At Ten... I'll Like You Again

©1998 by Just You & Me™
1st Printing, October 1998
2nd Printing, April 2001
3rd Printing, September 2005
4th Printing, July 2008

Just You & Me™
P.O. Box 639
San Luis Obispo, California 93406-0639
Phone/Fax: (805) 541-3515
www.justyouandme.com

Design by Ashala Nicols Lawler

Printed in China

ISBN 13: 978-0-9712675-4-1

Dedicated to my inspirations –
Jono and Michael
John
Kaci and Keli

You are my sunshine.

CONTENTS

MOMMY'S PLEDGE

*M*y beloved gift,
This child sent to me,
The lessons I teach you
Will affect who you'll be.

I'll acquaint you and guide you
And show you the way;
You are my sunbeam,
My golden ray.

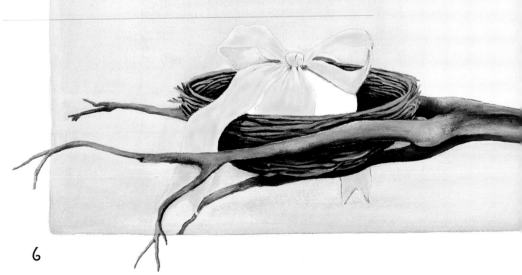

6

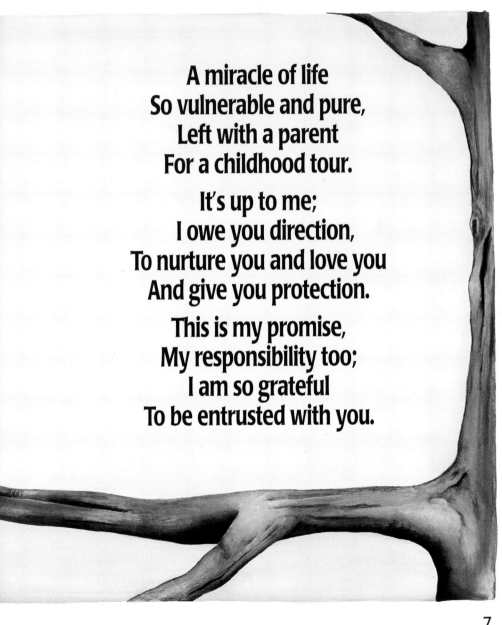

A miracle of life
So vulnerable and pure,
Left with a parent
For a childhood tour.

It's up to me;
I owe you direction,
To nurture you and love you
And give you protection.

This is my promise,
My responsibility too;
I am so grateful
To be entrusted with you.

8

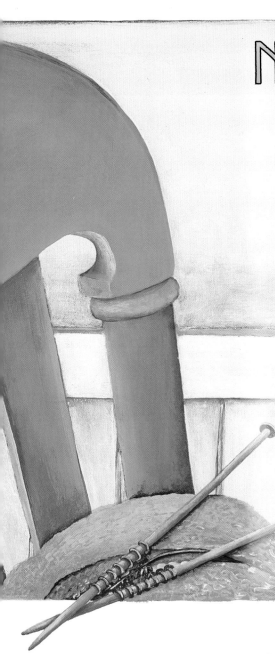

NEWBORN

*T*he day you arrive
I thank God above,
My precious angel,
My bundle of love.

Ten tiny fingers,
Ten tiny toes,
Eyes full of wonder
And a cute little nose.

Wrapped in a blanket
Made from grandma's yarn,
My heart is full
As you lie in my arms.

Entrusted to me,
I'll give you my best;
A bright future for you
Is my quest.

I hold you often,
Both asleep and awake,
If this is spoiling
I'll indulge for our sake.

I listen as you sleep
In the still of the night;
I hear your sweet breathing
And know you are all right.

9

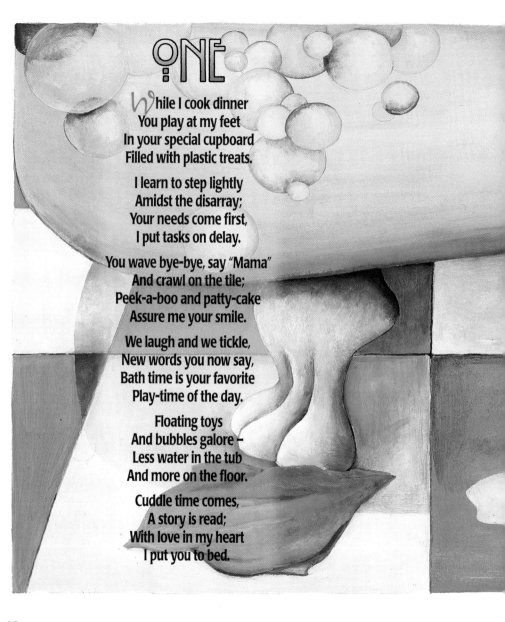

ONE

While I cook dinner
You play at my feet
In your special cupboard
Filled with plastic treats.

I learn to step lightly
Amidst the disarray;
Your needs come first,
I put tasks on delay.

You wave bye-bye, say "Mama"
And crawl on the tile;
Peek-a-boo and patty-cake
Assure me your smile.

We laugh and we tickle,
New words you now say,
Bath time is your favorite
Play-time of the day.

Floating toys
And bubbles galore –
Less water in the tub
And more on the floor.

Cuddle time comes,
A story is read;
With love in my heart
I put you to bed.

11

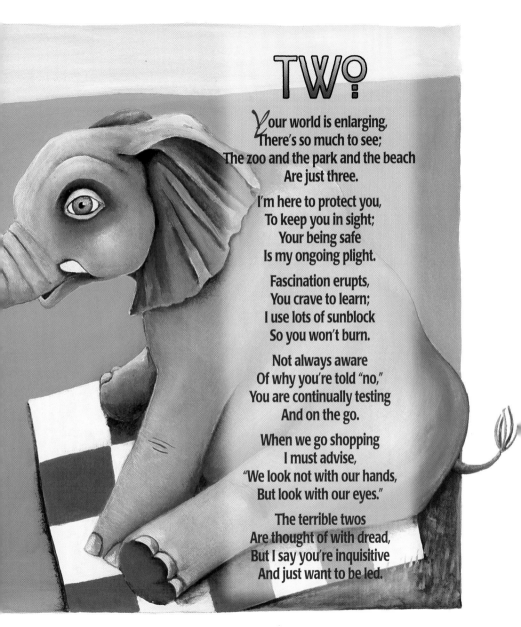

TWO?

Your world is enlarging,
There's so much to see;
The zoo and the park and the beach
Are just three.

I'm here to protect you,
To keep you in sight;
Your being safe
Is my ongoing plight.

Fascination erupts,
You crave to learn;
I use lots of sunblock
So you won't burn.

Not always aware
Of why you're told "no,"
You are continually testing
And on the go.

When we go shopping
I must advise,
"We look not with our hands,
But look with our eyes."

The terrible twos
Are thought of with dread,
But I say you're inquisitive
And just want to be led.

THREE

Don't talk to strangers,
You must comprehend;
I give you a warning,
Not all grown-ups are friends.

I teach you about manners
And when to be polite,
But I also enlighten you
When saying "no" is all right.

You discover responsibility,
You master a first chore;
You learn to put your toys away
That are left on the floor.

When a bad mood
Comes into play,
Mr. Grouch is invented
So you can throw it away.

Once in a while
You are out of control,
Three minutes of solitude
Takes on a role.

Your personality blossoms
More and more each day;
I like who you are
And all that you say.

FOUR

We continue to share
Quiet reading time each day,
Imagination and ideas
Are making their way.

A foundation is laid
For the school years ahead;
Homework time will replace
The time that I read.

I'm here to escort you,
To show you the way,
To guide you and teach you
And to hear what you say.

Traditions are born
In each family with time;
Eating together
Is a favorite of mine.

Now old enough to partake
In the meal's preparation,
Cooking together is fun
And adds to the creation.

We practice good manners,
Discuss events of the day;
We laugh and we learn
And have lots to say.

FIVE

School begins,
It's with a sigh,
This child of mine
Waves good-bye.

I cry your first day,
Much to my dismay;
This little person of mine
Is on their way.

Consistency with guidance
Is my role,
To be wishy-washy
Might take a toll.

Choices will be made
In the years ahead;
Your experiences will teach you
And direct where you're led.

I taught you about sharing
Not long ago;
This is today's lesson,
It's essential to know:

Do unto others
As you would expect,
It's important for you
To understand respect.

Dear Gran

SIX

The tooth fairy comes,
Front teeth are missing;
Your smile warms my heart,
You get extra kissing.

Grams and Gramps visit
With gifts from two;
You learn to send thank-you notes
And when they are due.

I show you my happy face
When yours is downcast;
I say "Corners up,"
Your frown doesn't last.

Your personality is fragile,
Just being conceived;
Praise and warm fuzzies
Are what you receive.

Whether it's academics, the arts
Or athletics you try,
Support, hugs and applause
Are given with pride.

Cold pricklies don't feel good,
Deflation is mean,
After all what's important
Is this child's self esteem.

SEVEN

*M*ore freedom and choice
Is given to you;
With this you have
More responsibilities too.

Chores are dispensed
To which you adhere;
You receive a dollar per week
For each of your years.

During the summer
When there is no school,
One book per week
Will give your brain fuel.

We discuss and review
The stories you read;
You also write letters –
I have planted that seed.

Our schedules are hectic,
We are busy with stuff;
But kid time is important,
I make sure there's enough.

We reserve special time
For just us two;
One-on-one talking,
It matters not what we do.

EIGHT

Your energy is high,
You are motivated to learn;
There's reading and writing
Even math has a turn.

Although no one person
Is better than the rest,
To succeed in this life
You must put forth your best.

We have a quiet time
Set aside for each evening;
You do your school work,
I do my reading.

I'm nearby
Should I need to assist,
But more help than that
Won't teach you the gist.

To some, learning is easy,
To some, it is not;
A parent must make sure
The child's not forgot.

I pay attention to signs
And HEAR what you say,
Your frustration in learning
Could turn to dismay.

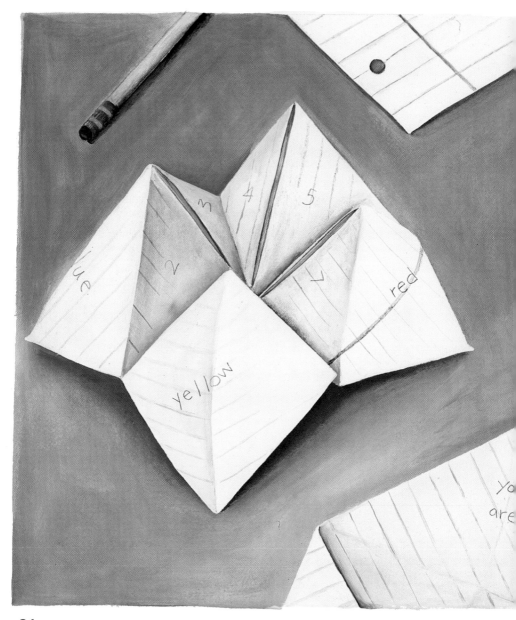

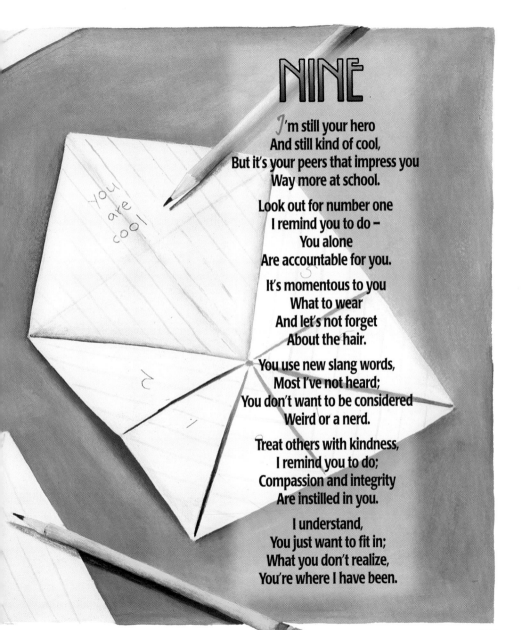

NINE

I'm still your hero
And still kind of cool,
But it's your peers that impress you
Way more at school.

Look out for number one
I remind you to do –
You alone
Are accountable for you.

It's momentous to you
What to wear
And let's not forget
About the hair.

You use new slang words,
Most I've not heard;
You don't want to be considered
Weird or a nerd.

Treat others with kindness,
I remind you to do;
Compassion and integrity
Are instilled in you.

I understand,
You just want to fit in;
What you don't realize,
You're where I have been.

TEN

Oh what a busy
Person you are
With all the friends
You have made so far.

When school is out
And more time to play,
You run inside and out
Of our house all day.

You have a sense of fun;
You laugh and smile;
Humor is a good trait
And a quality worthwhile.

You ride bikes or skate
Until it's nearly dark;
We play tennis and baseball
And fly kites in the park.

On rainy days
We get out the train,
Make fudge, eat popcorn
And play board games.

We go to the movies,
I take your friends too;
It's when you still like me
And I still like you.

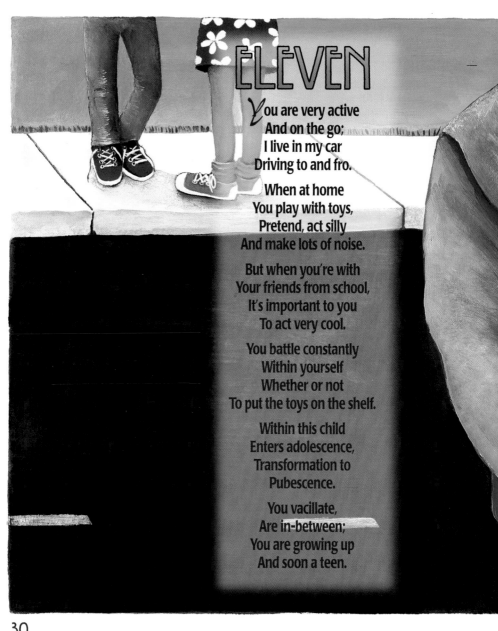

ELEVEN

You are very active
And on the go;
I live in my car
Driving to and fro.

When at home
You play with toys,
Pretend, act silly
And make lots of noise.

But when you're with
Your friends from school,
It's important to you
To act very cool.

You battle constantly
Within yourself
Whether or not
To put the toys on the shelf.

Within this child
Enters adolescence,
Transformation to
Pubescence.

You vacillate,
Are in-between;
You are growing up
And soon a teen.

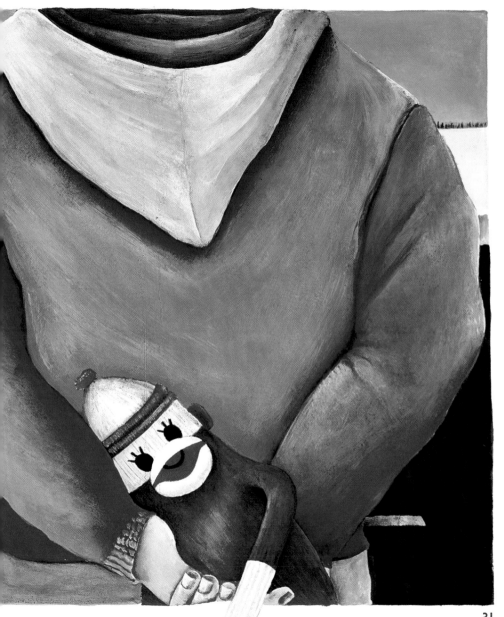

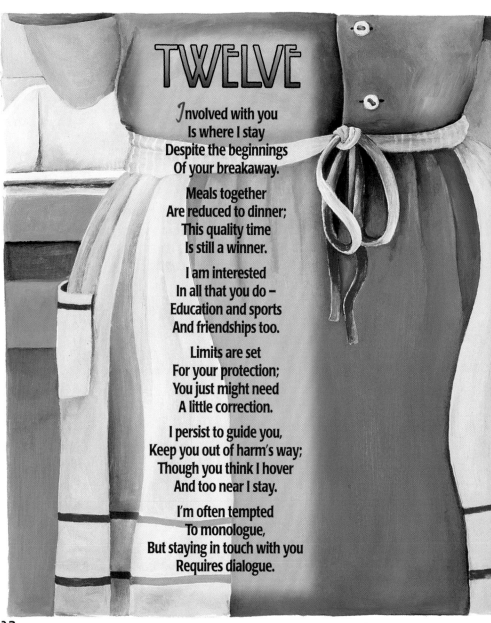

TWELVE

*I*nvolved with you
Is where I stay
Despite the beginnings
Of your breakaway.

Meals together
Are reduced to dinner;
This quality time
Is still a winner.

I am interested
In all that you do –
Education and sports
And friendships too.

Limits are set
For your protection;
You just might need
A little correction.

I persist to guide you,
Keep you out of harm's way;
Though you think I hover
And too near I stay.

I'm often tempted
To monologue,
But staying in touch with you
Requires dialogue.

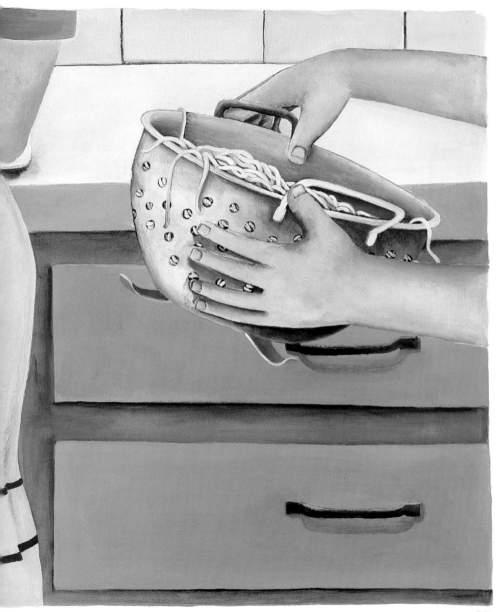

33

THIRTEEN

We listen to your music,
As we drive in the car;
I try to be open,
I'm glad it's not far.

I lend an ear,
I want to familiarize,
I make sure the lyrics
Are not those meant to despise.

Not all television programs
Are appropriate for you;
We watch some together
To discuss and review.

My personal interests
I'll not force on your core;
Pressing my passions on you
Might limit you for more.

You want to grow up
So very fast;
You say you know more
And that I live in the past.

The menacing generation gap
Is near
When my advice,
Is replaced by your peers'.

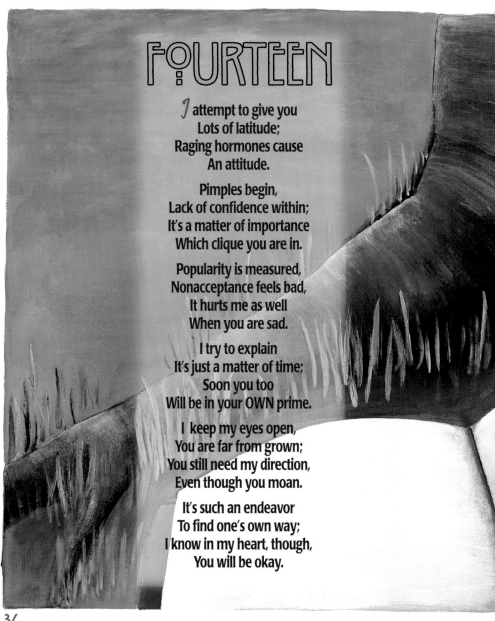

FOURTEEN

I attempt to give you
Lots of latitude;
Raging hormones cause
An attitude.

Pimples begin,
Lack of confidence within;
It's a matter of importance
Which clique you are in.

Popularity is measured,
Nonacceptance feels bad,
It hurts me as well
When you are sad.

I try to explain
It's just a matter of time;
Soon you too
Will be in your OWN prime.

I keep my eyes open,
You are far from grown;
You still need my direction,
Even though you moan.

It's such an endeavor
To find one's own way;
I know in my heart, though,
You will be okay.

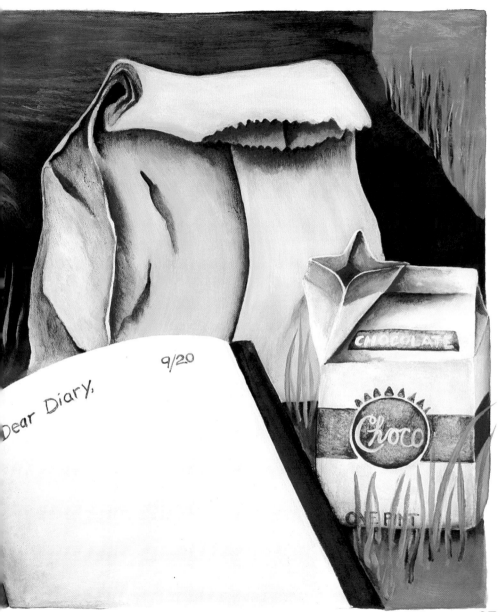

FIFTEEN

You push my buttons;
My engine starts –
My exasperation is showing,
Though I have love in my heart.

I try to have patience –
It comes from within;
This is not my strong suit –
I don't often win.

Friction between us
Runs extremely high;
My day often ends
With a good cry.

I praise ALL your good,
Forgive ALL your wrong;
I hope this phase you are in
Won't last too long.

The chores you are given
Are left undone;
You say that I nag
And act very dumb.

Then with a smile,
I recall where we've been;
I liked you at ten,
I'll like you again.

SIXTEEN

You play sports, go to parties
And drive a car,
But good grades and homework
Must be up to par.

Your social life
Is in full swing now,
It's MY prerequisite
To know with whom, where and how.

I preach drinking and drugs
Can mess with your head,
And to drive under the influence
Could leave someone dead.

Although I don't want to
Admit or believe,
There's a risk you'll experiment;
I will NOT be naive.

You often isolate
Behind closed doors;
Mutual respect
Is what I strive for.

A watchful eye
I endeavor to keep;
This limits your ability,
To get in too deep.

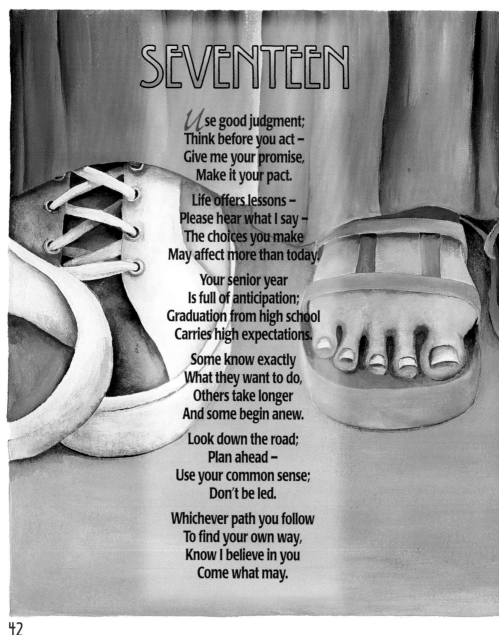

SEVENTEEN

*U*se good judgment;
Think before you act –
Give me your promise,
Make it your pact.

Life offers lessons –
Please hear what I say –
The choices you make
May affect more than today.

Your senior year
Is full of anticipation;
Graduation from high school
Carries high expectations.

Some know exactly
What they want to do,
Others take longer
And some begin anew.

Look down the road;
Plan ahead –
Use your common sense;
Don't be led.

Whichever path you follow
To find your own way,
Know I believe in you
Come what may.

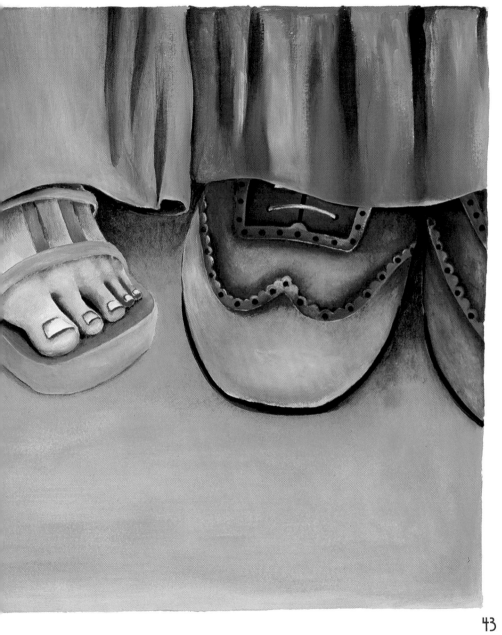

43

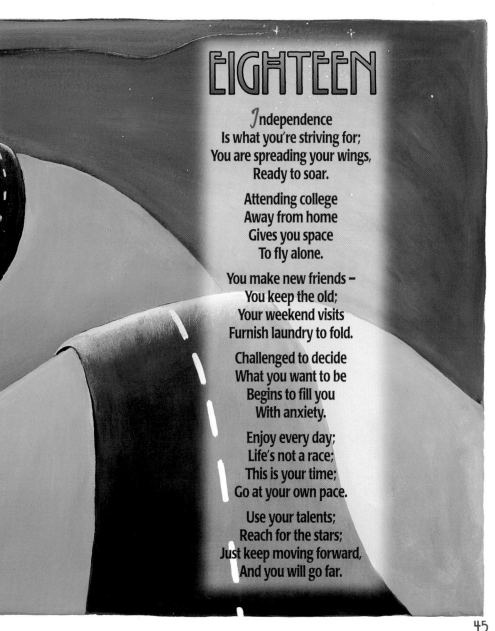

EIGHTEEN

*I*ndependence
Is what you're striving for;
You are spreading your wings,
Ready to soar.

Attending college
Away from home
Gives you space
To fly alone.

You make new friends –
You keep the old;
Your weekend visits
Furnish laundry to fold.

Challenged to decide
What you want to be
Begins to fill you
With anxiety.

Enjoy every day;
Life's not a race;
This is your time;
Go at your own pace.

Use your talents;
Reach for the stars;
Just keep moving forward,
And you will go far.

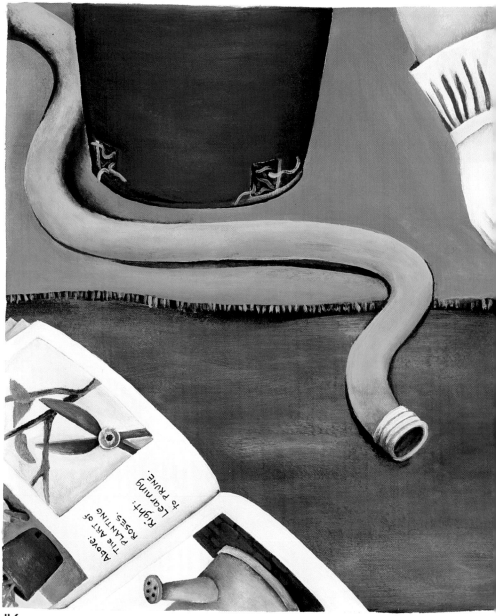

Above:
The Art of
PLANTING
ROSES.

Right:
Learning
to PRUNE.

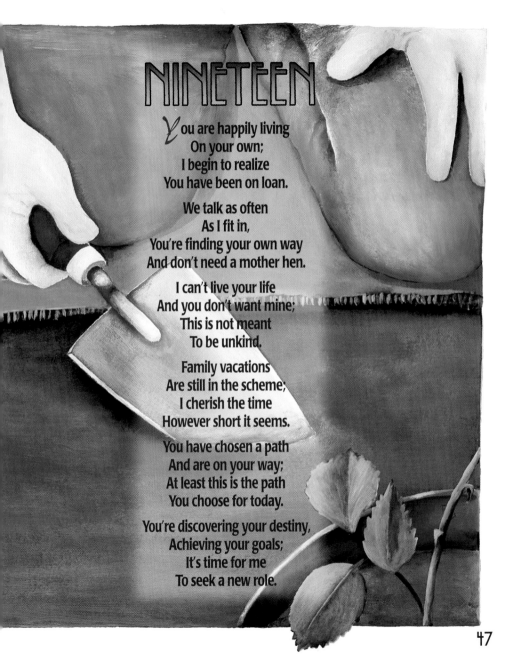

NINETEEN

You are happily living
On your own;
I begin to realize
You have been on loan.

We talk as often
As I fit in,
You're finding your own way
And don't need a mother hen.

I can't live your life
And you don't want mine;
This is not meant
To be unkind.

Family vacations
Are still in the scheme;
I cherish the time
However short it seems.

You have chosen a path
And are on your way;
At least this is the path
You choose for today.

You're discovering your destiny,
Achieving your goals;
It's time for me
To seek a new role.

TWENTY

*A*ll of a sudden
I'm sometimes right;
I'm not as dumb as I was,
Even last night.

Occasionally you ask
For my advice –
It had to be
At least once or twice.

It seems we have finally
Bridged our divide;
When we now talk
You even confide.

Losing sight of you
And all you can be,
Is oftentimes
A concern to me.

The devotion you have
For another
Turns your head towards
That significant other.

Don't let your affection,
And what it brings,
Sway you from YOUR goals
And deflate YOUR dreams.

TWENTY-ONE

We've shared your childhood,
You and I;
Now a young adult,
You are ready to fly.

The world is changing,
The future is yours;
Your zeal and diligence
Will open doors.

I've taught you the difference
Between right and wrong;
Your own life's lessons
Will succeed my song.

I had in my mind
Your destiny,
You did it your way,
As it should be.

I'm so very proud
To be your mother;
You warm my heart
As no other.

Stay true to yourself,
And follow your dreams;
I'm here for you always,
But you have been weaned.

REFLECTIONS

I encouraged you always
To reach for the sky
This same inspiration
To me applies.

With more dreams to realize
And places to see,
I look to the future
For lots more to be.

The days of yore,
I'll forever treasure;
The rewards you've given me
Cannot be measured.

You've brought me magic
And sunshine too,
Integrity and compassion
Were instilled in you.

My parental pledge
Is passed to you;
It's now your turn
To escort your child through.

By way of reflection
I offer you,
Hindsight with perception,
An insightful view.

When I reflect
Upon my mommy years,
My heart is warm;
I hold the memories near.

I'd hug you more,
Restrict you less;
My house might even
Be a mess.

Office work
Would have to wait,
I'd not come home
From work so late.

We'd read more books
And play more games;
I'd know all your friends
And their names.

I'd let go of
All the triviality
And concentrate
On the reality.

Unconditional love
Is the essential key;
Couple this with
Parental consistency.

If I could repeat
The years again,
This is ONLY
Where I would begin.

55

More books from...

Just You & Me™

For Kids You Love... And Grown-ups Who Care

Picture Book for Kids

Picture Book for Kids

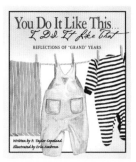

Keepsake for Grown-ups

Visit us at www.justyouandme.com... we'd love to hear from you.

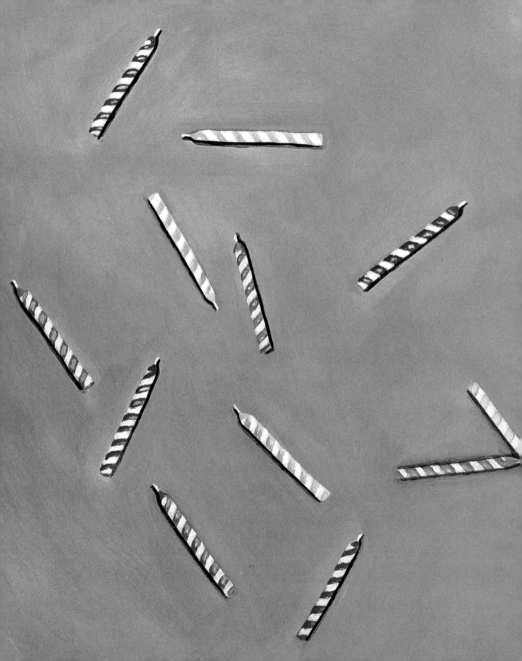